11/13

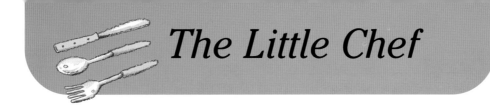

The Little Chef

Tasty Desserts
Little Chef Recipes

Author: Mercedes Segarra
Illustrations: Rosa M. Curto

Enslow Elementary
an imprint of
Enslow Publishers, Inc.

40 Industrial Road
Box 398
Berkeley Heights, NJ 07922
USA

http://www.enslow.com

Before You Start Cooking

1 Wash your hands with soap before you start working.

2 Wear an apron so your clothes will not get dirty.

3 If you have long hair, you can tie it back so it will not bother you while you cook, and no hair will fall into the food.

4 Before you start, read the recipe. Make sure you have all the necessary ingredients, and follow instructions step-by-step.

5 Weigh and measure all ingredients before you start cooking.

6 **Ask an adult** to help you turn on the oven or to cut ingredients with a sharp knife or scissors.

7 If you need to use the burners on the stove, please **ask an adult** to help you, too.

8 If you need to use the oven, it is a good idea to turn it on just as you begin the recipe so it will be hot when you finally need it.

9 Turn off the stove or the oven when you have finished using it.

10 Use pot holders to take pots, pans, or trays off the stove or out of the oven so you will not burn your hands.

11 Move the pot handles out of the way so you do not knock into them accidentally and drop them or burn yourself.

12 Clean the utensils as you cook. When you are done cooking, leave the kitchen as tidy as you found it.

Ingredients:

2 tangerines or 1 orange

1 small pineapple

2 bananas

8 strawberries

half a melon

honey

Fruit Skewers with Honey

1 Peel the tangerines and bananas. Pare the pineapple and melon.

2 Wash the strawberries and remove the leaves.

3 Cut the fruit into cubes.

4 Stick the different pieces of fruit onto the skewers.

5 Pour a little honey over the skewers.

5

Spring Dessert

Ingredients:

vanilla ice cream

clean strawberries

orange juice

a peppermint leaf

6

Instead of orange juice, you can also use some chocolate syrup.

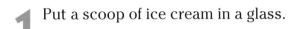**1** Put a scoop of ice cream in a glass.

2 Remove the leaves from the strawberries. Add a few strawberries and some orange juice to the ice cream.

3 You may add a peppermint leaf for decoration.

7

Ingredients:

strawberries

1 dark chocolate bar

1 white chocolate bar

8

Chocolate-Covered Strawberries

Make sure you use bowls that are microwave-safe.

1 Wash strawberries and remove leaves.

2 Break both white and dark chocolate into small pieces. Place each kind of chocolate in a separate microwave-safe bowl.

3 Microwave each bowl of chocolate for two minutes. You can also melt the chocolate using a double boiler.

4 Stir each bowl of chocolate with a wooden spoon. Dip a few strawberries into the dark chocolate and a few others into the white chocolate.

5 Leave the strawberries on a tray until the chocolate dries and hardens.

6 Place the strawberries in the refrigerator. Serve when they are cold.

9

Brownies

Ingredients:

1/3 cup of butter

5 ounces of semisweet chocolate

2 eggs

1 cup of sugar

1/3 cup of flour

1/4 cup of walnuts

1 Preheat the oven to 350°F. Beat the eggs and sugar until you get a smooth yellowish cream.

2 Melt the chocolate and butter in the microwave. Fold the chocolate into the eggs.

3 Add the flour and mix well.

4 Crack the walnuts, chop them, and add to the mix.

5 Grease the pan with a little butter, and sprinkle with flour.

6 Pour the batter into the pan, and spread it evenly.

7 Bake for 30 to 35 minutes.

8 After the brownies have cooled, you can serve them with vanilla ice cream.

 1.

 2.

 2.

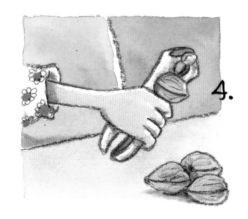 3.

 4.

 5.

 6.

30' 350°F

 7.

 8.

Cheesecake

Ingredients:

 1 package (8 ounces) of cream cheese

For the caramel:

 3 lemon-flavored yogurts (6 ounces each)

 3 tablespoons of sugar

 3 tablespoons of cornstarch (leveled)

 3 tablespoons of water

 3 eggs

3 1/2 tablespoons of sugar

You may also add a handful of raisins to the mix.

1 Pour water and sugar for the caramel into a microwave-safe glass container. Heat it in the microwave for about four minutes.

2 When the caramel starts becoming brown in color, take it out of the microwave and stir it.

3 Pour the caramel into a bowl. Add the cream cheese, yogurt, cornstarch, eggs, and sugar. Mix all the ingredients together until you get a very smooth cream.

4 Pour the mix back into the glass container.

5 Microwave it for 15 to 18 minutes. Let it cool.

6 Place it in the refrigerator to serve cold.

13

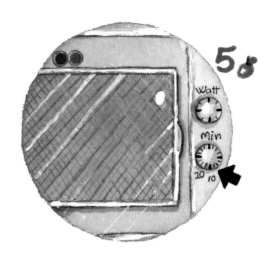

Ingredients:

1 watermelon

half a melon

2 pears

3 apples

2 kiwifruits

2 oranges

3 tablespoons of sugar

Watermelon Soup with Fruit Salad

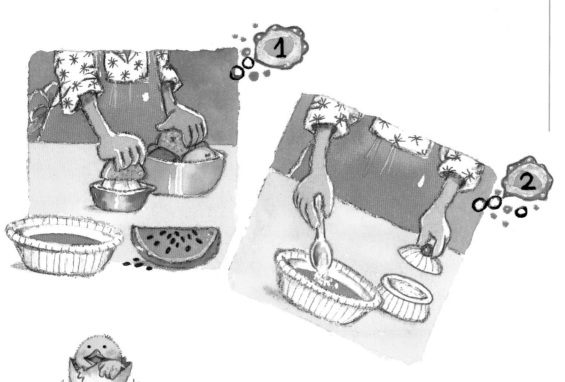

1 Scoop the watermelon pulp into a bowl. Squeeze the oranges. Crush the watermelon with a hand blender or regular blender. Add the orange juice. Pass it all through a strainer.

2 Add sugar and mix well.

3 Dice the other fruit. Add it to the soup.

4 Put it in the refrigerator to serve very cold.

You may dice any fruit in season that you like.

15

Strawberry Sherbet

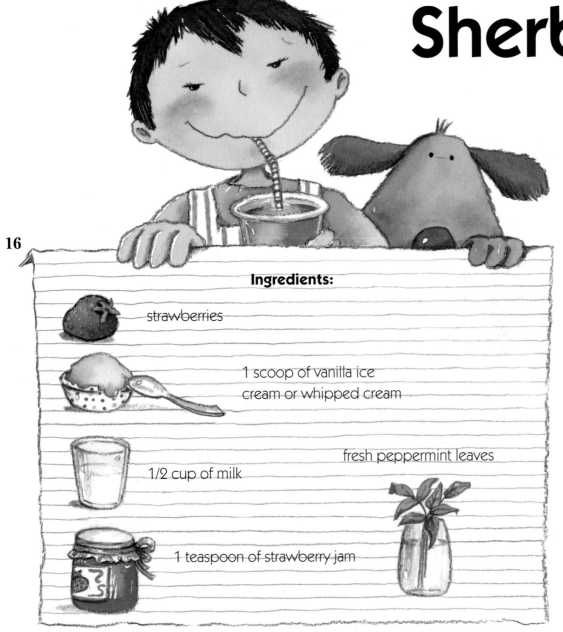

Ingredients:

strawberries

1 scoop of vanilla ice cream or whipped cream

1/2 cup of milk

fresh peppermint leaves

1 teaspoon of strawberry jam

1 Wash the strawberries and remove the leaves.

2 Put them in a bowl with the ice cream and milk.

3 Blend everything with a hand blender. You can also use a regular blender.

4 Add the jam.

5 Blend it again until you get a smooth cream.

6 Pour the sherbet into glasses, and garnish with one fresh leaf of peppermint.

Baked Apples

Ingredients:

6 apples

6 teaspoons of honey

6 cinnamon sticks

6 teaspoons of margarine

1 Preheat the oven to 350°F. Wash the apples and core them.

2 Place one teaspoon of honey, one cinnamon stick, and one teaspoon of margarine in the center of each apple.

3 Place the apples in a baking dish, and bake them for about twenty minutes.

4 You can serve the apples with some whipped cream on the side.

You may go to the supermarket with your parents and ask what kind of apples are best for baking.

Lemon Pie

Ingredients:

1 (12 ounces) can of evaporated milk

1 can (14 ounces) of condensed milk

about 30 ladyfingers

juice from 6 lemons

1 Squeeze the six lemons. Pour the juice into a bowl.

2 Add the evaporated milk and the condensed milk.

3 Mix well until you get a thick cream.

4 Place a layer of ladyfingers in a 10-by-10-inch baking pan. Cover it with the cream. Add a second layer of ladyfingers, and cover it again with the mixture. Make as many layers as necessary until the baking pan is full.

5 Set four to six ladyfingers aside, and crumble them to decorate the top of the pie.

6 Place the pie in the refrigerator for about ten hours.

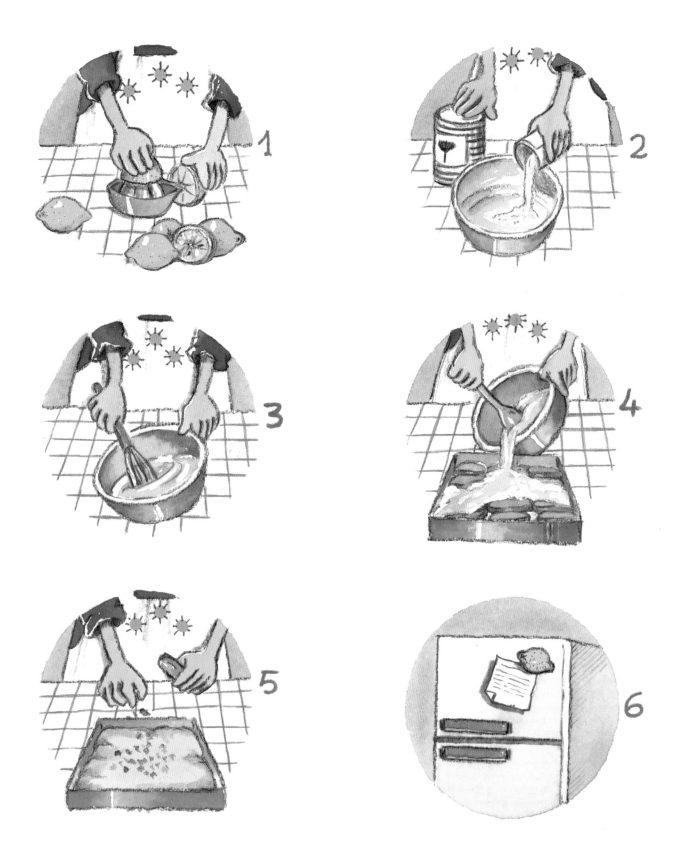

Chocolate Truffles

Ingredients:

3 1/2 ounces of
semisweet chocolate

2 tablespoons of butter

6 tablespoons of
condensed milk

grated chocolate
or cocoa powder

1 Break the chocolate into small pieces. Melt it in the microwave for about two minutes.

2 Add the condensed milk and butter, and mix well, stirring with a wooden spoon.

3 Place the batter in the refrigerator until it hardens (about six hours).

4 Make small balls with the hardened mix.

5 Roll the balls in the grated chocolate or in cocoa powder.

6 Place them in the freezer, and serve very cold.

It is easier to make truffles when the weather is cold because the mix turns soft when it is hot.

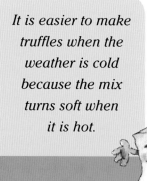

Apple Tarte Tatin

Ingredients:

1 tablespoon of butter

5 apples

1 sheet of puff pastry

For the caramel:

3 tablespoons of sugar

3 tablespoons of water

a few drops of lemon juice

To garnish:

chopped almonds

1 Preheat the oven to 400°F. Peel the apples, cut them into fourths, and core them.

2 In a skillet, fry the apples in butter for a few minutes until they are a golden color.

3 In a microwave-safe round mold, make the caramel with three tablespoons of sugar, three tablespoons of water, and a few drops of lemon juice. Heat it in the microwave until it turns brown.

4 Place the apples in the caramelized mold with the curved side down.

5 Lightly flour the puff pastry, and pierce it with a fork.

6 Place the puff pastry over the apples, and tuck the edges down around the apples.

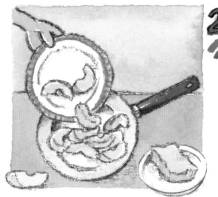

7 Bake until the puff pastry is brown (about thirty minutes).

8 After it cools, cover the tart with a dish, and flip the mold upside down. Decorate the tart with chopped almonds.

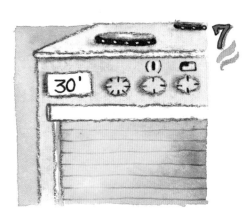

Yogurt with Wild Berries

Ingredients:

3/4 cup of raspberries

3/4 cup of blackberries

plain or vanilla yogurt

2 tablespoons of sugar

4 tablespoons of water

1 Put some yogurt in a bowl.

2 Wash the raspberries and blackberries.

3 Heat the berries in a pan, or microwave them, with four tablespoons of water and two tablespoons of sugar.

4 Pour some warm raspberries and blackberries over the yogurt.

26

1

2

3

4

27

You can also use ice cream instead of yogurt.

Walnuts with Cream and Banana

Ingredients:

4 tablespoons of sugar

4 tablespoons of water

a little bit of cooking oil

1 banana

1/2 cup of shelled walnuts

whipped cream

1 Fry the walnuts in a frying pan in a little bit of cooking oil.

2 When the walnuts are a little toasted, add the four tablespoons of sugar and four tablespoons of water.

3 Stir the walnuts with a wooden spoon until the sugar caramelizes.

4 Place them on a dish. After they cool a little, separate them using your fingers. They will be a little sticky.

5 Peel the banana and slice it.

6 Prepare a glass with some whipped cream, the banana slices, and a handful of walnuts.

Words to Know

squeeze

spread

melt in double boiler

peel

stick

fill

pot holder and kitchen towel

squeezer

refrigerator

scale

pot

frying pan

skewer

stir

separate

grate

cut

pour over

31

apron

grater

scissors

glasses

deep-freezer

pour

mash

fold in

boil

caramelize

bake

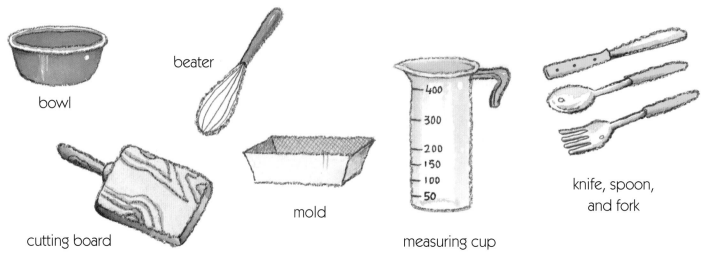

bowl

beater

cutting board

mold

measuring cup

knife, spoon, and fork

beat

melt

unmold

garnish

line

heat

colander

glass

hand blender

burners and oven

tray

containers

Read About

Books

Price, Pam. *Cool Cookies and Bars: Easy Recipes for Kids to Bake.* North Mankato, Minn.: Checkerboard Library, 2010.

Time for Kids: Kids in the Kitchen Cookbook: 101 Recipes for Kids to Make! New York: Time for Kids, 2013.

Tuminelly, Nancy. *Cool Cake and Cupcake Food Art: Easy Recipes That Make Food Fun to Eat.* North Mankato, Minn.: Checkerboard Library, 2011.

Internet Addresses

Disney Family.com: Recipes for Kids
<http://family.go.com/food/pkg-cooking-for-kids/>

KidsHealth: Recipes and Cooking
<http://kidshealth.org/kid/recipes/>

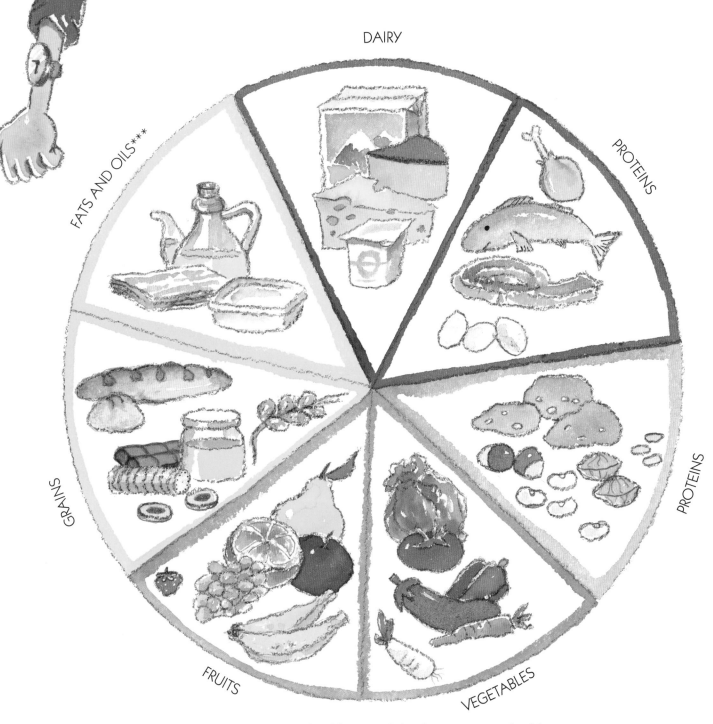

There are five basic food groups. You should eat food from each food group to stay healthy:

- **Fruits:** apples, bananas, berries, fruit cocktail, 100% fruit juice, grapes, oranges, peaches, pineapple
- **Vegetables:** broccoli, carrots, celery, corn, cucumbers, lettuce, peppers, potatoes, spinach, squash, tomatoes
- **Grains:** bread, cereal, crackers, grits, noodles, oatmeal, pasta, rice, tortillas
- **Proteins:** beans, beef, chicken, eggs, fish, lamb, nuts, peas, pork, seeds, shellfish, tofu, turkey, veal
- **Dairy:** cheese, milk, soymilk with added calcium, yogurt

***You need to have some fats and oils to be healthy, but not a lot.

WARNING: The recipes in this book contain ingredients to which people may be allergic, such as nuts.

To Our Readers: We have done our best to make sure all Internet addresses in this book were active and appropriate when we went to press. However, the author and the publishers have no control over and assume no liability for the material available on those Internet sites or on other Web sites they may link to. Any comments or suggestions can be sent by e-mail to comments@enslow.com or to the address on the back cover.

Enslow Elementary, an imprint of Enslow Publishers, Inc.
Enslow Elementary® is a registered trademark of Enslow Publishers, Inc.

English edition copyright © 2014 by Enslow Publishers, Inc.

Original title of the book in Catalan: *PASTISSOS I POSTRES*
Copyright © GEMSER PUBLICATIONS, S.L., 2003
C/ Castell, 38; Teià (08329) Barcelona, Spain (World Rights)
Tel: 93 540 13 53
E-mail: info@mercedesros.com
Web site: http://www.mercedesros.com
Author: Mercedes Segarra
Illustrator: Rosa Maria Curto

Library of Congress Cataloging-in-Publication Data

Segarra, Mercedes.
  Tasty desserts : little chef recipes / Mercedes Segarra.
    pages cm. — (The little chef)
  Audience: 7-8
  Audience: K to grade 3
  Summary: "Includes thirteen recipes for desserts, such as brownies, cheesecake, and strawberry sherbet, a 'before you start cooking' section, and an illustrated vocabulary list"— Provided by publisher.
  Includes bibliographical references.
  ISBN 978-0-7660-4261-2
  1. Desserts—Juvenile literature. 2. Cooking—Juvenile literature. I. Title.
  TX773.S3547 2013
  641.86—dc23
                                    2012031115

Paperback ISBN 978-1-4644-0465-8
Printed in China
122012 Leo Paper Group, Heshan City, Guangdong, China
10 9 8 7 6 5 4 3 2 1